which is to be found on the librarian's desk. In the case of this book, the details to be recorded are:

It is important that these details be copied exactly.

5. No book marked "For Reference Only" may be removed from the library, except by arrangement with the librarian.

Victorian London

Stella Margetson

Contents

5   Introduction

9   Victoria's reign

27   Victoria's capital

49   Londoners at home

73   The London streets

91   Art and learning

109   Victorian amusements

© London Weekend Television Ltd. Macdonald & Co. (Publishers) Ltd. , 1969 . SBN 356 02713 9

First published in 1969 by Macdonald & Co. (Publishers) Ltd.,St. Giles House, 49 Poland Street, London W.1

Made and printed in Great Britain by William Clowes & Sons Ltd., London and Beccles

fifty years of

Victorian London

from the Great Exhibition to the Queen's death

by Stella Margetson

Macdonald, London

A cheap fish vendor in St Giles.

Introduction

The London Queen Victoria inherited in 1837 was a prosperous, elegant city with some very dark and sleazy corners and not much sanitation, but a city without a sprawl, surrounded by the green fields of Middlesex and Surrey, where such villages as Hampstead, Islington and Dulwich dozed in the bright morning air. The London the Queen left behind in 1901 was a giant metropolis stretching like an octopus to Hornsey and Tottenham in the north, to Streatham, Croydon and Sydenham in the south, with millions of chimney-pots pushing a thick layer of smoke into the sky, miles of underground sewage pipes, a network of railways and occasionally to be seen in the streets that odd and outlandish curiosity the horseless carriage, driven by an electric or a petrol engine.

It was a city of violent contrasts—of great splendour and luxury, of shocking poverty and despair; of cunning and boisterous cockney behaviour and of sober, middle-class gentility. It was a city bursting with vitality and in the minds of most of its inhabitants forever progressing towards a bigger and better future, where industry, honesty and self-help, combined with reverence for church and chapel, would receive the rewards of the just, and laziness, improvidence and corruption be punished by the law. Year after year the bricks and mortar piled up in an orgy of neo-Gothic, pseudo-classical and industrial grandeur, smothering the gracious Georgian past and mauling the wonderful conception of John Nash and the Prince Regent. London was the central focus of the new urbanization of the people. Its streets were not paved with gold, but it was the magnet, the heart of a nation that had turned from agriculture and home industry to mass production, and of a nation whose Empire coloured the map of the world red.

There was nothing that could not be bought or sold in London; nothing from the Far East, from Africa or the new world across the Atlantic that did not find its way to the docks in the Port of London, where the grey waters of the Thames swirled round the hulls of the new steamships destined to travel the oceans of the world. Merchants, bankers, insurance agents, market-men, stock jobbers and their army of clerks, endlessly writing in a neat italic script in big, dusty ledgers, worked long hours in the City. In the West End and the new suburban centres, the shopkeepers vied with each other in the variety of their display: Mr Whiteley in Bayswater called himself the 'Universal Provider', Mr Derry united with Mr Toms in Kensington. The 'carriage trade' was cossetted and encouraged; money prudently invested yielded dividends to be spent on new comforts.

At the top of society after the death of the Prince Consort and the withdrawal of the Queen into perpetual mourning, the Prince of Wales and the Marlborough House set ruled the fashionable world. London was gay with balls and receptions and the Season was observed with as much assiduity as a tribalistic ritual. The nobility paid court to His Royal Highness, the bankers paid his debts and were rewarded by invitations to the royal box at Covent Garden. At the bottom of society lay the amorphous, shifting population of the underworld: the thieves and prostitutes, the down-and-outs muffled in rags asleep on the seats of the new Victoria Embankment and the half-starved urchins hopping in the gutter.

Aesthetically the expansion of Victorian London was a disaster, for it happened to coincide with an alarming degeneration of taste. Mass production, made possible by the inventive skill of the manufacturers in the Midlands and the North, was partly responsible for this; the sudden wealth of the parvenu industrialists as opposed to the declining influence of the cultured aristocracy another factor. Public buildings were on a grand scale; the bigger and the more pompous they were the more they displayed the power and the prestige of the British Empire, the high ideals of the church and the strength of the City as the most important trading centre in the world. Private building was for the speculators, some of them good, some very bad indeed; or for the institutional bodies aware of their duty to construct schools, hospitals and dwellings for the working classes. Faced with a population explosion from 1,500,000 in 1830 to over

4,500,000 in 1900, the Victorian Londoners had no alternative but to build and to go on building.

There were architects and engineers of genius, whose achievements reached the highest level and whose work we still cherish and admire: the Houses of Parliament, the Royal Opera House, Tower Bridge, St Pancras and the market halls at Smithfield, Covent Garden and Leadenhall. But perhaps the most noble of the Victorians' achievements, considering the pressure put upon them by the size of the metropolis they had begun to develop and could not stop, were their efforts to save a few open spaces in the odd and unregarded corners of their city. The Royal Parks were sacrosanct. Even the plans for the Great Exhibition in Hyde Park were changed to build the Crystal Palace round the elm trees on the site instead of uprooting them. Hampstead Heath was saved from the speculative builder by public subscription in 1872, Battersea Park laid out between 1850 and 1858; and in countless development schemes from Peckham to Kilburn, large or small areas with a few iron seats under the dusty trees were designated Victoria Park or Queen's Park for the benefit of the neighbourhood's inhabitants.

The Victorians were practical too. They tackled the immense tasks of administration, sanitation and health rather late, but with determination. They put their faith in the policeman with his truncheon as a protection against riot and disorder. They extended the street lighting, so that everywhere in the twilight and the fogs, the gas-lamps gave comfort to the pedestrian. They had crossing-sweepers, who made a clean path for the top-hatted and crinolined gentry stepping from one side of the street to the other, and they laid straw outside the houses of the well-to-do when anyone was ill and could not stand the clatter of the traffic.

Victorian London was an amalgam of light and dark. In this picture book we have tried to show you some aspects of its energetic and absorbing life.

George Cruikshank's view of the enormous crowd that flocked to London in 1851 for the Great Exhibition. The Exhibition, magnificently housed in the Crystal Palace, was impressive testimony to Britain's booming industry and trade.

The Archbishop muddled up the orb and the sceptre; otherwise the Coronation in Westminster Abbey went off very well. Outside in the bright sunshine Londoners waited for their new Queen to reappear through the great west doors and enter her gorgeous golden coach with its royal scarlet trappings. Victoria was not a beauty, but she had a fresh pink and white complexion and compared to the late King William IV with his brandy-coloured face and his gouty feet, she was a romantic figure. The crowds were profoundly moved by her air of innocence and her youth. 'The scenes of enthusiasm, affection and loyalty were really touching,' she wrote in her diary when she got home to Buckingham Palace. And after she had laid aside her royal robes, she gave her beloved little dog Dash his bath.

Eighteen months later the same crowds jostled behind the guardsmen lining the route from Buckingham Palace to the chapel at St James's, where the Queen in white satin was united in marriage to her cousin Prince Albert of Saxe-Coburg-Gotha. The Prince was handsome, high-minded and very correct. The English aristocracy found him inexplicable. He did not care for fox-hunting; he preferred botany. He did not gamble or drink heavily, or ogle the maids of honour; he liked privacy and playing the organ. But whatever the aristocracy thought, before long the Teutonic Prince had conquered the English Queen. She adored him. She not only began to rely entirely on his wise advice in matters of state; she gave up dancing and all her girlish, giddy behaviour to find, as she wrote in her diary, '*real* and solid happiness' in the quiet domestic life they enjoyed together with their growing number of children.

By 1851 Prince Albert's taste and his influence had penetrated far beyond the Royal Household. The Great Exhibition he sponsored in Hyde Park, 'uniting the industry and art of all the nations of the earth', was a triumphant success. Joseph Paxton's brilliantly designed Crystal Palace of prefabricated iron and glass, three times the length of St Paul's and covering some nineteen acres of ground, presented a dazzling spectacle and was filled with 'myriads of wonderful things': marble statues, and a stuffed elephant from India, ornate pianos, Gothic furniture, a chair made out of a lump of English coal, knick-knacks of papier mâché and mother-of-pearl, and all the engineering wonders of the Industrial Revolution. Thackeray described the opening ceremony as 'a noble awful great love inspiring sight, much grander than a coronation', and the Queen, deeply moved by the joy expressed in every face, wrote: 'God bless my dearest Albert and my dear country, which has shown itself so great to-day.'

London was packed to suffocation. Six million people visited the Exhibition; 900,000 Bath buns were consumed on the premises and over 1,000,000 bottles of lemonade. Very early in the proceedings the Prince had decided to prohibit the sale of alcoholic refreshments in the restaurants, and it was observed that the industrial classes behaved with 'manifest propriety and good temper'. Thomas Cook ran hundreds of excursion trains from the provinces, clergymen brought their parishioners in parties from the remote country and school-teachers hordes of children in button boots and sailor hats. The effect of the Exhibition was to widen the horizon of the lower and the middle classes and to make London known to thousands of people who had never seen it before.

But ten years after his great achievement, the Prince, exhausted by his incessant toil for the good of the nation and shocked by his eldest son's peccadilloes at Cambridge, fell ill and died quite suddenly. The Queen's grief was alarming. 'There is no one to call me Victoria now,' she lamented. 'I only lived through him, my heavenly Angel.' Henceforth she withdrew from public life and made a fetish of her mourning, preferring Balmoral, Windsor and Osborne to London. Yet she faced her duty as Queen with courage and a royal devotion.

Lord Palmerston was her Prime Minister at the time, a veteran in politics, who had waltzed at Almack's in the dissipated days of the Regency. He was a bold, uninhibited English gentleman with a will of his own that had crossed the

Queen's earlier in her reign, and a furious, insular attitude towards foreigners backed by the power of the British navy. After the death of the Duke of Wellington in 1852, he was Britain's elder statesman, hated and feared by some and respected by others. It was cruelly said that when his wife Emily forgot her rouge and he omitted to dye his whiskers, a real crisis in the affairs of the nation could be expected, but he ruled with great authority until 1865.

Gladstone succeeded Palmerston as leader of the Liberal party and became Prime Minister in 1868. The Queen disliked him. She complained that he spoke to her as if she were a public meeting and in spite of his wife's advice 'to pet her a little', he never succeeded in gaining her confidence. He argued with her interminably and she mistrusted his radical ideas. Yet he was responsible for a great deal of useful reform in England and in his private life a man of the highest probity. Even his nocturnal rambles about the streets of London had a moral purpose, for it was his habit to pick up the prostitutes in Mayfair and take them home to his wife in Carlton House Terrace, where she strove to make them see the error of their ways.

Disraeli's gift for pleasing the Queen was quite a different matter. He was an elderly widower when he became Prime Minister for the second time in 1874, as old and as wily as the Orient from which his Jewish ancestors had come, with a yellow face and dyed hair, a subtle smile and a brilliant brain. He knew exactly how to flatter the Queen by appealing to all that was most romantic in her nature; and after thirteen years of loneliness and despondency, she blossomed again at the age of fifty-five like the primroses she picked at Osborne and sent to him in a moss-lined box with the royal coat of arms embossed on the lid. She created him Earl of Beaconsfield, he made her Empress of India. He bought the Suez Canal for her with the Rothschilds' money and when he returned from the delicate negotiations at the Congress of Berlin, which saved England from a costly war with Russia, he gave her the credit for his achievement.

It was his last gesture. The Queen's cares multiplied after his death. Gladstone vexed her more than ever; Lord Salisbury was more to her liking. The conduct of the Prince of Wales was very disquieting; both the Mordaunt divorce case and the Tranby Croft scandal of cheating at cards involved the heir to the throne in the wrong sort of publicity. Then there was trouble in Africa, in both the Sudan and the Transvaal; and trouble at home, where one Sunday in 1887, the police had to call in the Guards to help them suppress crowds of angry demonstrators fighting for the right to hold public meetings.

Yet the Queen's Jubilee in that same year and her Diamond Jubilee in 1897 were both celebrated with fervour and delight. As she drove through the decorated streets of London at the centre of a magnificent procession, her small head nodding and her plump hand waving to her loyal subjects, their enthusiasm warmed her heart. Not many of them had seen her Coronation; she had outlived most of her generation. And London had changed greatly; it was bigger, more crowded, with new buildings everywhere that were quite bewildering. But she had seen her beloved Albert immortalised forever in the princely Memorial poised in Kensington Gardens his figure seated beneath an elaborate Italian Gothic *baldacchino* pointing eternally towards the sky and the Continents of the world lying at his feet.

The Queen knew nothing, except by report, of the wild scenes of rejoicing in London after the Relief of Mafeking; the Boer War distressed her and she did not live to see the end of it. She had only one more journey to make through the streets of London when her coffin was borne on a gun-carriage from Victoria to Paddington Station, with her eldest son and her grandson, Kaiser Wilhelm, riding behind it and every Londoner from the youngest child to the oldest inhabitant clothed in black. It was not only for the stout old lady with the obstinate mouth that the people mourned, but for a way of life which had made London the biggest and most prosperous city in the world.

Right, an engraving based on a photograph of Prince Albert. Earnest and industrious, the Prince's qualities were never appreciated by the British.

Far right, Victoria and Albert in 1854, after 14 years of marriage. The Queen, a devoted and dependent wife, retired into nearly 30 years of sorrowful seclusion after the Prince's death in 1861.

Right, Lord Palmerston, the dominating figure in British politics from 1846–65. During this period, he vigorously promoted British rights and interests abroad by a policy of 'gunboat' diplomacy.

Far right, Bloody Sunday, November 13, 1887, when a demonstration in Trafalgar Square organized by the Social Democratic Federation to assert their right to hold public meetings was brutally dispersed by the Life Guards.

Below, a cartoon at the time of the Reform Bill of 1884, which extended household suffrage to the country constituencies. It depicts Gladstone leading Franchise into the train while Lord Salisbury as a porter gives a helping hand to Redistribution.

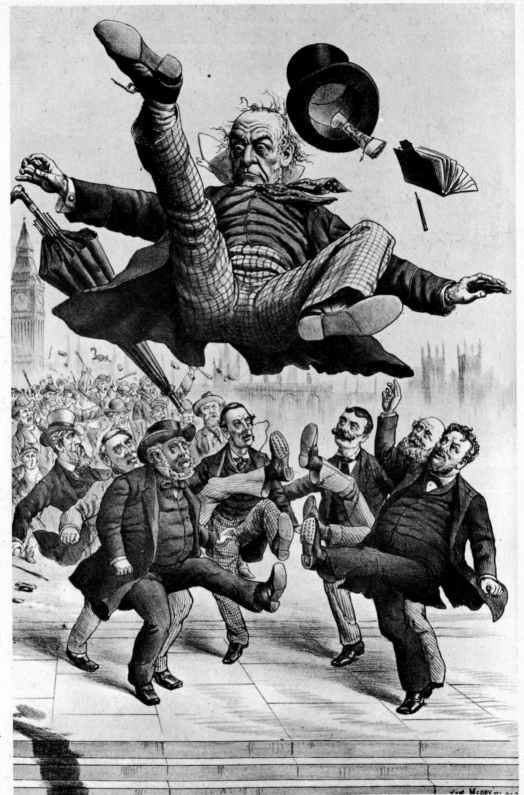

Right, John Bull and his friends kicking Gladstone sky-high for his advocacy of home rule for Ireland – a highly unpopular proposal that cost him the election of 1868.

Far right, William Ewart Gladstone, the Grand Old Man of British politics who transformed the old Whig party into the new Liberal Party by a series of long overdue reforms.

Right, a cartoon of 1870 showing Disraeli (dressed as an Indian merchant) presenting the Queen with the imperial crown of India.

Far right, Benjamin Disraeli in 1878. Twice Prime Minister, he pursued a policy of spirited intervention in foreign and imperial affairs.

Below, the Diamond Jubilee procession in 1897. Both jubilees proclaimed the greatness of Britain's new Empire, of which the only official link was the Queen herself.

Right, Queen Victoria in 1887, Golden Jubilee Year. In old age, the Queen, having emerged from her long seclusion, was a popular and respected figure.

Right, the Prince of Wales (later Edward VII) in the 1880s. Allowed little responsibility by the Queen, he devoted himself instead to the gay life of high (and not-so-high) society.

Far right, the Queen's funeral procession in February 1901 led by Edward VII followed by the Kaiser (the Queen's grandson).

*Fleet Street, looking eastwards
to St Paul's, crammed with traffic
as dense as that of today.*

Many of London's most famous landmarks were built in the reign of Queen Victoria.

Sir Charles Barry's superb design for the new Palace of Westminster, with its glorious frontage on the river, its towers and pinnacles of pale limestone and its romantic inner courts, was an inspiration which justified the whole of the Gothic Revival in architecture. G. E. Street's Law Courts in the Strand rose up like a vast cathedral, the great interior hall lending dignity to the ancient ritual of the law. Sir Gilbert Scott's St Pancras startled the eye of the beholder by its size and grandeur. But when it came to rehousing the Foreign Office, Palmerston told Scott he wanted 'none of your damned Gothic', he wanted 'a sumptuous Renaissance Palace'—and he got one, which when seen from the lake in St James's Park with the Horse Guards and the skyline of Whitehall Court beyond forms one of the most marvellous urban landscapes in the world.

In the City the neo-Gothic and the pseudo-classical vied with each other in the streets that still followed the pattern of London's history. The new Royal Exchange was built in the classical style, the immense pile of offices for the Prudential Assurance Co. in red-brick Gothic. Bankers leaned towards a classical pomposity, merchants towards a Gothic magnificence that expressed their respectable endeavour to unite the worship of Mammon with the worship of God. The approach to St Paul's was ruined by the Ludgate Hill railway bridge, the gulf of Farringdon Street brilliantly accented by the bold sweep of Holborn Viaduct. The narrow alleys and courts, where the chop-houses, taverns, barbers and bookshops abounded, were darkened by the size of the new buildings. The huddle of ancient houses in Clerkenwell and Cloth Fair remained.

The new market halls at Smithfield, Leadenhall and Billingsgate, with their cast-iron pillars and high concave roofs designed on the principle of Paxton's Crystal Palace, were masterly. But perhaps the most remarkable Victorian building of all was the Byzantine Moorish temple with its scrolled ironwork, cruciform interior and great oriental dome designed for the Sewage Pumping Station at Abbey Mills. This was the above-ground monument to the enormous underground sewage system that was forced on the administration after the cholera epidemic of 1848 by Sir Edwin Chadwick, an ardent reformer and commissioner of the Poor Law, and carried out by a team of navvies under the Chief Engineer to the Metropolitan Board of Works, Sir Joseph Bazalgette.

The same extraordinary mixture of styles marked the development of the rest of London as the urban needs of the people began to eat up the market gardens of Brompton, the farms of Earls Court and the fields around Belsize Park. The rich built their private palaces, Stafford House, Bridgewater House and Dorchester House, in a classical style of great splendour. Thomas Cubitt and his imitators in Belgravia and elsewhere built stately rows of cream-coloured terrace houses with steps up to a classical portico, large windows, high ceilings, cavernous basements and narrow attics for the servants, while wealthy land-owners, like those of the Cadogan estate, leased sites to speculators working in the ponderous and highly elaborate Gothic baronial style.

The middle classes, as public transport improved, spread out in all directions —to Balham, Tooting, Herne Hill, Catford and Beckenham. The streets they lived in conformed to the pattern of their incomes, ranging from the grandiose to the more modest and to those who eked out a frugal existence in genteel poverty, 'keeping up appearances' above the jungle of the lower orders. An enormous variety of new building materials came into use for their suburban homes: red, yellow and purple bricks, Cornish granite, Welsh slate and stone from Yorkshire while for the purposes of exterior decoration terracotta medallions and friezes were fabricated in the factories as well as majolica and faience tiles, synthetic stone and marble that was not marble at all.

Churches proliferated in the suburbs as in the more central districts, where Butterfield built his stupendous All Saints, Margaret Street, with a passionate intensity of feeling. Wesleyan and Baptist chapels multiplied with non-conformist severity. Somewhere to accommodate the dead and their commemoration in stone had to be found—acres at Norwood, Brompton and Highgate. Some attempt was made to preserve more rural surroundings for the living in the smaller, semi-detached villas with gardens in Camberwell and St John's Wood.

Meanwhile the poor lived in the seething, rat-infested rookeries of the East End, St Giles's, Clare Market and a score of other districts where the old houses had fallen into ruin and the new 'back-to-backs' were rapidly degenerating into slums. The mammoth task of rehousing these people in less squalid surroundings was left to private benefactors. The immensely rich Baroness Burdett-Coutts built a vast Gothic square of tenements in Bethnal Green in 1859 and the generous American philanthropist George Peabody, who spent more than £400,000 on improving the conditions of the London poor, put up his first modern block of 'model dwellings' or working-class flats shortly afterwards. Almost as grim and as functional as the Victorian warehouses beside the docks, the Peabody Buildings were highly praised; baths were installed in the basements—without any hot water.

But private charity, however munificent, was not enough. Almshouses for the aged, Rowton Houses for the homeless and hospitals for the sick might be endowed by the guilty conscience or the benevolence of the rich but the prisons had to be renewed and maintained by the State: These included Newgate, one of the oldest, Pentonville, as strong as a baronial castle, and Holloway, no less severe and covering ten acres. Not all the poor were 'deserving'. There were the gambling dens, the gin palaces and pubs with their gaudy gas-lights where the criminal instinct fed on vice or misery could be drowned in a drunken orgy.

Yet in spite of the misery, the streets of London were full of sharp contrasts in character, of cockney humour and boundless energy. The rigid class structure that prevailed in private life broke down a little in the crowded thoroughfares.

Oxford Street and Regent Street might be full of carriages bringing the ladies of Belgravia in to do a morning's shopping and the obsequious shop-walkers in Peter Robinson's be clothed in frock coats, but the bottle-nosed bus drivers, the hell-for-leather cab drivers, the tired shop assistants and the modest seamstresses were there too, with the errand-boys weaving in and out and the delivery vans holding up the traffic. Occasionally a horse bolted or the scarlet fire-engines galloped into action. London smelt of horses and horse dung.

West End or East End, the streets and the open spaces teemed with life. The gentry paraded in Hyde Park after church, the cockney took his family off to Hampstead in his cart with a lump of sugar in his pocket for the pony. The muffin-man rang his bell outside the respectable houses in Kensington, the street doctor did a roaring trade with his Elixir of Life pills. The lamp-lighter leaving his moons of light in the street below the high nursery windows of Bayswater comforted the little girl going to bed and outside the sleazy lodging-houses not far away in Paddington signalled to the prostitute that it was time for her to start on the prowl. The policeman walked his beat in silent boots and the maidservants waited for him by the area railings.

There were railings everywhere—round the public conveniences with their tiled stairs leading down from the street, round the gardens in the squares where the plane trees nodded in the afternoon and the upper-class children bowled their hoops—railings with spikes and wrought-iron patterns, repeated in the coal lids covering the cellars in front of the houses. Decorative art ran riot in all the street furniture. Pillar-boxes, invented by the novelist Anthony Trollope, had lids like lotus flowers, lamp-posts were fluted like Corinthian columns, horse troughs sculpted to look like Roman sarcophagi, iron seats curved into contortions with lions' feet and a sphinx to support the arms. The Victorians dreaded simplicity; they yearned for elaboration to prove to themselves that what they were doing was right and proper.

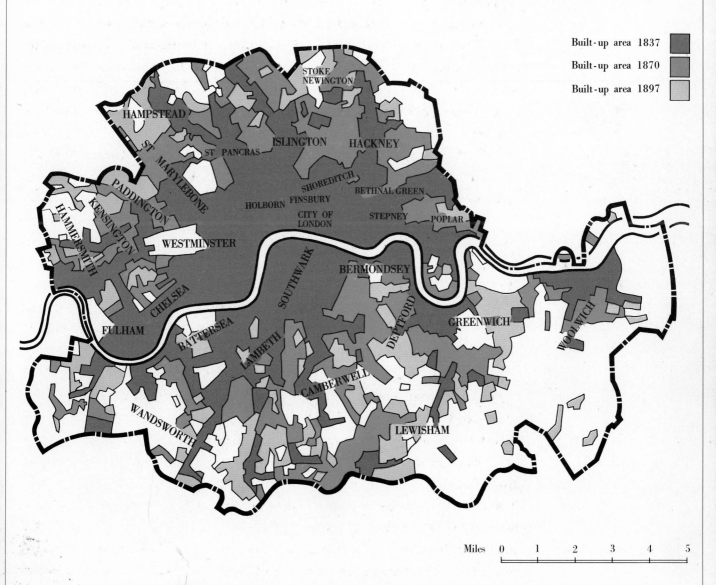

Victorian London

Built-up area 1837
Built-up area 1870
Built-up area 1897

HAMPSTEAD

STOKE
NEWINGTON

ST MARYLEBONE

ST PANCRAS

ISLINGTON

HACKNEY

PADDINGTON

SHOREDITCH

HAMMERSMITH

KENSINGTON

HOLBORN FINSBURY

BETHNAL GREEN

WESTMINSTER

CITY OF
LONDON

STEPNEY

POPLAR

CHELSEA

BERMONDSEY

FULHAM

BATTERSEA

SOUTHWARK

DEPTFORD

GREENWICH

WOOLWICH

LAMBETH

CAMBERWELL

WANDSWORTH

LEWISHAM

Miles   0   1   2   3   4   5

Below, Cheapside decorated for
the Diamond Jubilee in 1897. In
the background is the Royal
Exchange, one of many grand
Victorian buildings in the City,
in this instance in a classical style.

Right, dilapidated old houses in
Cloth Fair – one of the dismal
slum spots that survived in the
City off the broad commercial
thoroughfares. Thousands
continued to live in squalid
surroundings during the 19th
century.

Right, a large Victorian terrace house in Queen's Gate, South Kensington. Such tall, imposing residences, their basements and attics inhabited by servants, were the homes of the prosperous upper-middle class.

Far right, a view from St James's Park of the Foreign Office (designed by Sir Gilbert Scott). Scott's first designs in a Gothic and a Byzantine style were rejected by Palmerston, who insisted on a classical building.

Right, a doorway in Cowan Street, Camberwell, one of Victorian London's fastest growing suburbs. The top-heavy capital, with its cluster of crude foliage, is a typical decorative flourish.

Far right, houses in Sandover Road, Camberwell, a debased late-Victorian version of the terrace house, hideously and unnecessarily decorated with fancy brickwork and plaster mouldings.

Below, porters at Covent Garden,
photographed in 1877, then
already for two centuries London's
main fruit and vegetable market.

Right, Smithfield Market, built in
1868, an outstanding example of
Victorian ironwork construction.
Like many industrial buildings
of the period, its design owed much
to Paxton's Crystal Palace.

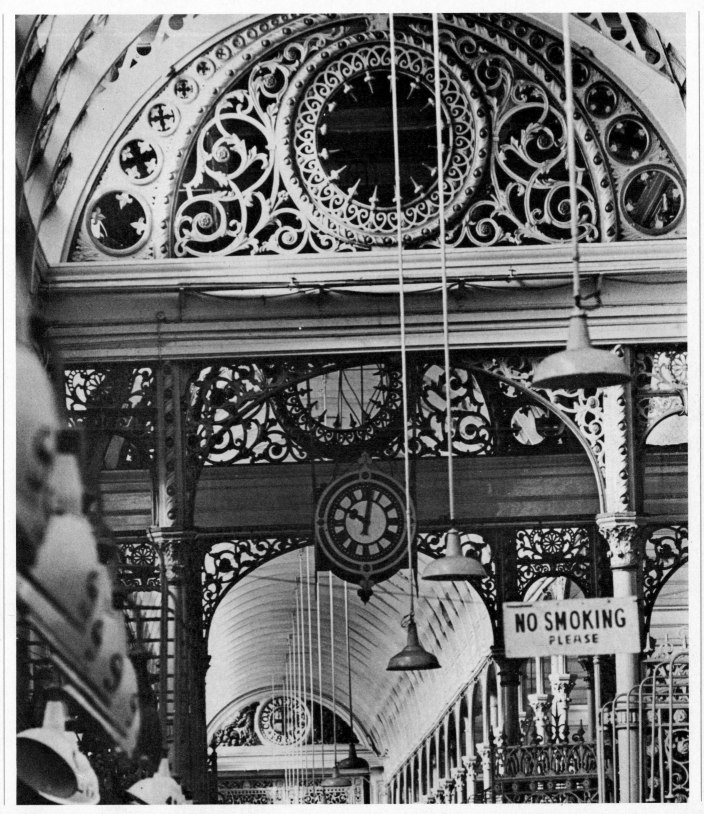

Right, the Albert Memorial, Sir Gilbert Scott's elaborate and imposing monument to the Prince's zealous promotion of learning and the arts.

Far right, Peabody Buildings in Clerkenwell. The American philanthropist endowed several blocks of 'model' dwellings for the working class, which though bleak and comfortless were a great improvement on the crowded and insanitary 'rookeries'.

41

Right, the muffin-man, a familiar
and welcome sight to children
returning to tea in Kensington or
Bayswater after a walk in the Park.

Far right, a hawker of patent
medicines displays his wares.
Street traders offered an enormous
range of goods for sale and all
day long the streets resounded
with their cries.

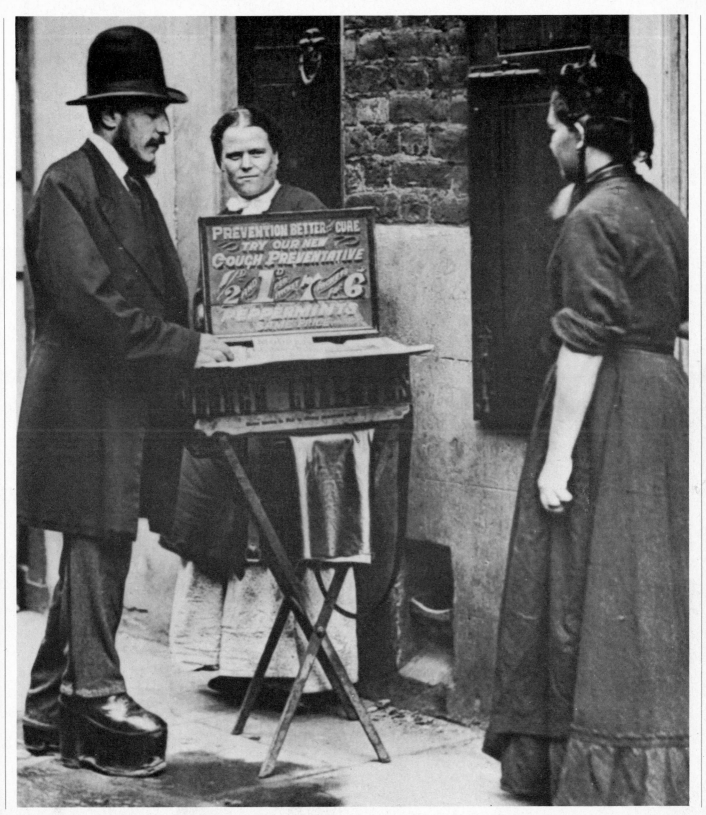

Right, Victorian warehouses at Wapping, whose stark functionalism contrasts with the highly ornate domestic architecture of the time.

Far right, the amazing Byzantine interior of Abbey Mills, one of four pumping stations constructed as part of Bazalgette's new system of main drainage begun in 1859.

Right, a Victorian pillar-box in St John's Wood, decorated with a typically elaborate finial and royal cypher.

Far right, fire engines in Bread Street in 1899.

A scene outside an old furniture shop in the 1870s; it vividly conveys the poverty of working-class life.

Life in Victorian London was sharply divided on three different levels: the rich, the middle classes and the near destitute.

The rich nobility lived in great luxury in their splendid mansions in Park Lane, Arlington Street and Piccadilly. They came to London for the Season from their estates in the country. Some of the gentlemen held office in the Government, some of the ladies attended the Queen They were Society: a closed circle, aristocratic, formal, demanding. Their dinner-parties, musical entertainments, balls and receptions glittered; their carriages, their fashionable clothes, their jewellery all displayed authority and exclusiveness. Etiquette was a straight-jacket and the marriage market an intricate game of patience played by the patrician mamma with four or five daughters to dispose of, none of whom could be allowed to marry 'beneath her' or to remain a spinster. The well-to-do, high-bred mother of Florence Nightingale was horrified when she found her daughter passionately studying medical text-books quite 'unfit for feminine eyes' instead of being content to wait for an eligible suitor.

But after the Queen's retirement from public life, some of the more rigid restrictions on Society began to decline. Birth was no longer quite so important. The gay Prince of Wales liked his friends to be rich, but was not quite so particular where he found them as long as they were amusing and gave lavish parties, where the food and the drink and the fat cigars were of the best quality and the ladies of an attractive appearance. For a time Mrs Langtry ruled him with her cold eyes and her beautiful hour-glass figure and became so much the rage of London that people stood on chairs in the Park to get a glimpse of her driving by in her open carriage. Hyde Park in the Season was one of the 'interesting and imposing sights' recommended to foreign visitors by Herr Baedeker in his first guide to London. It showed off the grandeur of English Society to perfection.

An army of servants—butlers, footmen, coachmen and the like—ministered to the nobility and, in a less exalted fashion, to the needs of the middle classes. Among them, keeping a manservant and a carriage was a status symbol, which gave the household an upper-class air of extravagance. But most families were content to hire a carriage and to employ a female staff—a cook at £20 a year, a head parlourmaid, housemaid and several tweeny-maids to run up and down-stairs between the basement and the top-floor nurseries. Servants worked hard, endlessly carrying copper hot-water cans up and down, scrubbing floors, blacking grates, cleaning the brass and even the wallpaper with bread, and it was not until the end of the century that the vacuum-cleaner came in to assist them. Yet in a well-run household, they were better off, better fed and much cosier than the match girls or the sewing women who scraped a living in the factories.

The influence of the Queen and Prince Albert had a profound effect on middle-class family life. Their decorum was imitated in countless London homes. and respectability was the highest prize of a well-regulated life. While papa went off to the City in his top-hat and frock-coat, mamma stayed at home to manage the servants, order the meals, water the plants in the conservatory and watch that the children behaved themselves—unless, of course, she was lying on the sofa recovering from her last confinement or expecting another. Families were large. Prosperity bred children one after the other, often as many as twelve or thirteen, and women did not complain. Though papa was the breadwinner and the god, mamma was the ultimate ruler of her domestic domain.

She had Mrs Beeton's invaluable book on *Household Management* to help her with the economical planning of her menu, with the making of jam and pickled walnuts and the best way to get rust off a steel fender. And for light reading she had books from nice Mr Mudie's Lending Library, though it was rather shocking when he started circulating those dreadful novels by Ouida. She had her embroidery, her bead-work, her fine sewing and the marvellous clutter of all the things she loved around her: the chenille cloth with bobbles on it, the overmantel draped and crowded with photographs, bric-à-brac, vases and china; the little tables for work-baskets, tea-cups and albums; her wax fruit under glass, her fire-screens and lamp-holders, chairs with frills to hide their legs and pictures in porcelain of the dear Queen and Prince Albert.

Upstairs the bedrooms were equally cluttered and much colder—no fires after May 1, even if a north-east wind was blowing through the streets of Bayswater. Soon there were bathrooms and W.C.s with mahogany seats and surrounds and a brass handle to pull. Comfort was everything. When papa came home from the City his slippers were warming by the fire and his velvet jacket was hanging in his dressing-room ready to put on. He seldom discussed his business affairs; no woman's mind could be expected to grasp her husband's work at the Bank of England or Lloyd's, and if he happened to be 'in trade' he might be slightly ashamed of it, though, of course, 'the wholesale' was more respectable than 'the retail', at least until the end of the century when the barriers were falling fast.

Papa romped with his children at bedtime or read aloud to them in the evenings and home entertainments were part of their lives. Apart from their dolls and their rocking-horses, they had magic lanterns and a machine called a stereoscope with a velvet covered eyepiece and hundreds of cards that fitted into a movable frame at the end of it and gave a striking third dimension to pictures of the Taj Mahal or the Charge of the Light Brigade. And there was always the piano with its fretted front and twisted candelabra for mamma and the girls to play and sing to. Life was based on a somewhat pious and sentimental family affection that could become a tyranny. Sunday was a bleak day, with a morning visit to church, no afternoon amusements and a cold supper at night to give the servants time to go to Evensong. But religious belief suffered a shock from which it never wholly recovered when Darwin published his *Origin of Species* and Huxley his studies in scientific theory.

The lower middle classes in the less prosperous suburbs of Kennington or Tooting did their best to ape the upper middle classes of Sydenham and Norwood. Both lived in their own tight little world of gentility, respectability and privacy. Neither of them saw much of the underside of London, or if they saw it, they lacked the imagination to comprehend it. They did not know—or preferred not to know—that whole families as big as their own were living in one basement room in Bermondsey with the paint peeling off the walls and no plumbing. They never saw the porters at Covent Garden sweating under a load of baskets piled high on their heads in the early morning or the women at Billingsgate up to their elbows in slippery, wet fish.

And the people in work were the lucky ones. They could buy bread and some scrag-ends of meat to put in a stew for Sundays and second-hand clothes at the market stalls in the street, whelks and winkles or tripe for their supper and fried fish wrapped up in a greasy newspaper. The men could pick up a bit mending chairs or shining shoes and selling chestnuts up West, or heaving coals and moving garbage. But the old were haunted by the horror of ending up in the workhouse and the barefoot children in rags picked up what they could find in the gutter. Much was done to relieve their distress, but what was done was never enough, and only a few of the hale and hearty with a taste for adventure were bold enough to look for the recruiting sergeants with the Queen's shilling, standing outside the pubs to hook their meat for the army.

London spread, London grew. One half of its inhabitants did not know how the other half lived. Yet there was not much envy or class hatred. Social climbing and social snobbery belonged to the middle classes and the wealthy. Cockney stamina and cockney wit armoured the poor against their troubles; their robust mockery often succeeded in making their lives more tolerable when the good intentions shown towards them by the genteel classes failed. After all, London was theirs—they had nothing else.

A middle-class Victorian family gathered around the tea table. Family life, modelled on that of the Queen, was decorous and respectable, governed by an inflexible code of moral and social behaviour.

Below, a young lady of the 1880s
enraptures three admirers with her
playing. Music was a common
form of entertainment ranging
from elaborate musical evenings
to a few songs round the piano.

Right, a fashion plate of 1877.
During the seventies, ladies'
fashions took on an almost 18th-
century look with swathed skirts;
these later developed into the
extravagant bustles of the 1880s.

Right, a fashion plate of the 1890s showing how narrower and more manageable skirts had superseded unwieldy bustles and crinolines of earlier decades.

Far right, a photograph of the 1860s showing a crinoline being lowered over the wearer's head.

Below, some of the servants found in any well-to-do household. They are: the groom, the gardener, the 'boots', the gardener's boy; the cook, the parlourmaid, the housemaid and the 'tweeny'.

Right, part of a Victorian doll's house, which gives us a glimpse of the layout and furnishing of a typical middle-class home.

Right, an advertisement guaranteed to appeal to the Victorian love of cleanliness. Servants scrubbed and polished continuously, particularly in London with its pall of grime.

Far right, a patriotically named baby with her nurse in about 1891.

A contrast in baby minding: right, a homeless mother and baby on the workhouse steps and, far right, Gladstone with a child on his knee.

Right, a middle-class family stiffly posed in their Sunday best.

Far right, a scene outside a London pub in the 1870s. Drinking was often the working man's only recreation.

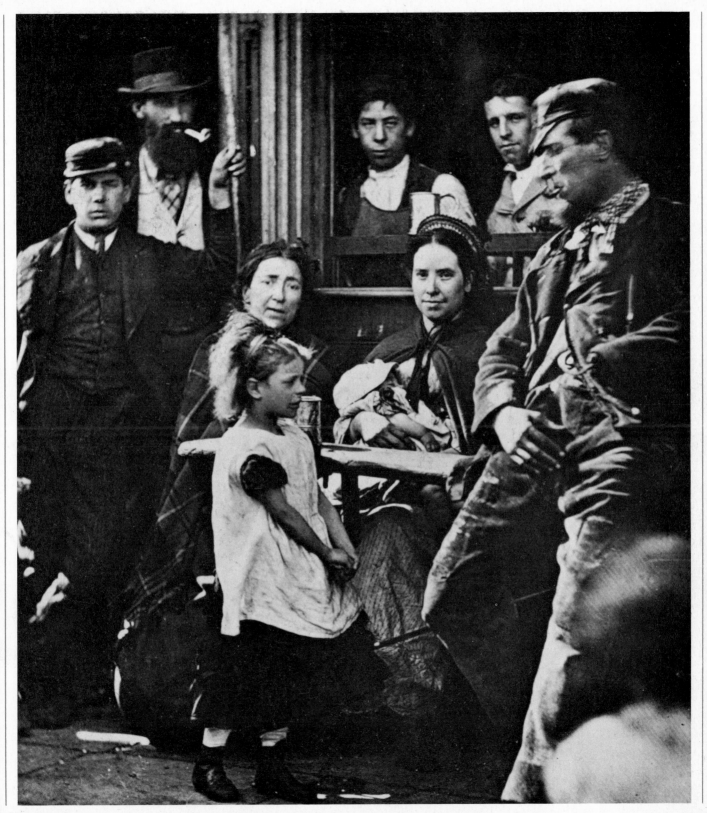

Right, Charles Darwin, whose
Origin of Species *(1859), by
undermining belief in the Bible,
started a bitter controversy between
Faith and Science that raged for
thirty years after the book's
publication.*

*Far right, the interior of All
Saints, Margaret Street (1859),
by William Butterfield. A
prominent Gothic Revivalist,
Butterfield was noted for his rich
decoration, particularly his use of
coloured brick.*

Right, a soldier leaves his wife for the South African front in 1899.

Far right, recruiting sergeants at Westminster in 1877. Army life, despite its dangers, sometimes seemed preferable to a miserable existence in the slums.

A knifeboard bus (that is, with back-to-back rooftop seats) in its final form about 1895, complete with brakes, a rear platform and a curving staircase.

The dramatic developments in rail transport from the 1840s onwards were both a cause and an effect of the colossal expansion of Victorian London. Just when the mail and stage coaches after 200 years of evolution had reached their height and were second to none in the world for speed, smartness and efficiency, the 'tea-kettle' engine arrived and the genius of George Stephenson, Matthew Boulton and Isambard Kingdom Brunel sparked off a revolution. The great coaching inns in the City and their West End offices in Piccadilly from being the busiest and most highly organized centres of transport in Britain were suddenly deserted. Travelling by rail was faster, cheaper and the new thing. Jane Carlyle was terrified by the prospect and thought she would be certain to faint on her first journey. Instead she found 'no difference between the motion of the steam carriage and the stage coach' and called it travelling 'by air'.

Before long the roads of Britain no longer echoed with the music of the guard's horn. A network of iron rails, tunnels, viaducts and railway stations covered the countryside and George Hudson, the 'Railway King', was making a fortune. London was the centre of attraction, the point where the railway lines converged. Engineers and architects rivalled each other in constructing giant railway stations with all the paraphernalia of train sheds, glass-roofed platforms, iron bridges, goods yards, booking-offices, waiting-rooms and refreshment-rooms for the ever increasing numbers of passengers. Euston, Waterloo and London Bridge were established in the forties; King's Cross and Paddington in the fifties; Charing Cross, Victoria and St Pancras a decade later.

All the most modern technical devices and all the most advanced skills in architectural design were brought into use: glass and iron at Paddington by Brunel and Digby Wyatt, classical vaulting at King's Cross by Lewis Cubitt, Gothic splendour at St Pancras by Sir Gilbert Scott. At Paddington it was guaranteed that the engines would 'consume their own smoke and steam', but this did not work out in practice and the Ecclesiastical Commissioners who owned the surrounding land, discovered that the gentry refused to occupy the new houses they were building in Westbourne Terrace on account of the noise of the shunting engines and the stench from their funnels.

The comfort of the gentry was considered first in the design of the railway carriages, which became ever more luxurious with hanging lights, armchairs or sofas, dining-cars and kitchens to serve them. Queen Victoria's royal saloon was fitted out like a drawing-room with satin curtains, a rich carpet and a quilted ceiling. The second-class and third-class passengers naturally did not fare so well; for a long time the latter were carried in open trucks with sparks from the engine flying backwards over their heads and all the discomfort of exposure to the elements, but this made no difference to the popularity of the cheap excursion trains.

Experiments to link up the termini by means of the Metropolitan Railway, built on the 'cut and cover' principle, were successfully completed in 1863 when the first line from Paddington to Farringdon Street was opened; and very soon other lines were extended to serve the suburbs, where modest little stations were erected in the still rural surroundings of Finchley Road and Willesden Green. The carriages were lit by gas carried in iron bottles, which had to be replenished at intervals, but this and the noxious fumes from the engine in no way deterred the stout-hearted Londoners who found the new railway highly convenient. By the end of the century the 'Twopenny Tube' had arrived and electrification of all the underground railways was being considered.

Yet far from easing the traffic problems above ground, the various local railways, by increasing the numbers of people in the metropolis, added to the fearsome congestion in the streets. London Bridge in the morning was packed with vehicles of all kinds, hay-carts, brewers' drays, horse buses, private broughams and victorias, cabs and pedestrians. The City, where formerly merchants and other businessmen used to live above their work, was now crowded in the daytime and almost empty at night. Those who did not come in by rail travelled by horse bus, a vehicle invented in 1829 by George Shillibeer 'after the manner of the recently established French *omnibus*'. The first of them seated eighteen passengers inside, but soon the 'knifeboard' was devised by Thomas Tilling to carry as many passengers as could be wedged in together on the top deck after ascending by a runged ladder and later by an outside stairway fitted with a 'decency board', which made it possible for ladies to climb on top without exposing too much leg. The horse trams in South London carried even more people and for those who could afford it, there were the hackney-carriages, the growlers and the 'gondola' of London, the two-wheeled hansom cab.

With all this explosion of traffic it became obvious that improvements were urgently needed in the central districts if London were to maintain its ascendancy as the greatest capital in the world. And here again, as with the sewers, it was Sir Joseph Bazalgette who as Chief Engineer to the Metropolitan Board of Works set about reorganizing and replanning the streets. His most splendid achievement lay in reclaiming acres of mud from the Thames to construct the Victoria Embankment linking Blackfriars Bridge with Westminster, the Albert Embankment opposite the Houses of Parliament and the Chelsea Embankment farther upstream. But to link the Victoria Embankment with Trafalgar Square, the last of the great patrician houses of old London belonging to the Dukes of Northumberland was ruthlessly torn down to make way for Northumberland Avenue, a street lined with ponderous new luxury hotels, the Grand and the Metropole, and pompous buildings which housed various clubs and the Turkish Baths, open to ladies as well as gentlemen at a fee of 4s.

The Metropolitan Board of Works also cut a road northwards from Trafalgar Square (Charing Cross Road) to link up with Tottenham Court Road and Shaftesbury Avenue, another new street named after the philanthropic earl, who had fought so persistently to improve the conditions of the poor. The monument raised to him in Piccadilly Circus in the nineties was intended to be 'a symbol of Christian charity', but was crowned with Alfred Gilbert's Eros, the god of love, so that with the Piccadilly 'Flower Girls' in their straw hats and shawls sitting round it, the London Pavilion Music Hall on one side and the Criterion Hotel and Restaurant on the other, it became instead the hub of London's nightlife and the focus of the gay man about town in his opera hat and cloak.

In the City and the East End new streets were cut through to the docks, which were deepened and extended to take the new iron ships as big as the Great Eastern. The Royal Victoria Dock was built in 1855, the Prince Albert in 1880, with huge warehouses for storing grain and over 1,000,000 carcasses of meat from overseas. The Thames had long since ceased to be the most convenient way for the Londoner to get about; no one any longer 'went by water to Vauxhall' as Pepys had done. But the Victorians renewed the old bridges all the way along it or erected new ones. Thomas Page designed Westminster and the Chelsea Suspension Bridge; Bazalgette built Hammersmith, Putney and Battersea; and Sir Horace Jones and Sir John Wolfe-Barry created one of the most spectacular of all London's landmarks in 1894 when they completed Tower Bridge at a cost of £1,500,000.

No one took the new horseless carriages appearing in the streets very seriously. They were rather a joke, a new sport for the rich. Yet there were fanatics among the pioneers of the motor-car who worked hard for the repeal of the Locomotive Act of 1865, which required a man or a boy with a red flag to walk in front of 'all vehicles propelled by any power other than a horse or an ox'. This they achieved in 1896 and celebrated their victory by organizing the first London to Brighton run starting from the Hotel Metropole in Northumberland Avenue. Three years later there were six taxi-cabs licensed for hire, standing outside the Hotel Cecil in the Strand. Revolutions have a way of creeping up on London unobserved.

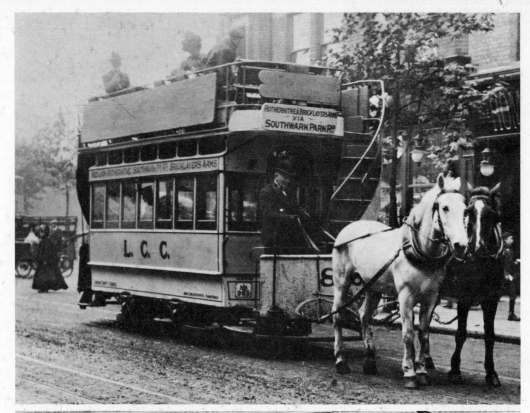

Top right, a London tram in the late 1890s. Double-deck horse-trams ran on suburban routes in South London only from 1870; they were taken over by the L.C.C. in 1898.

Bottom right, an example of a knifeboard bus introduced about 1851 and originally owned by Thomas Tilling. Seating 24 people, it was the first bus to run in London with passengers on the roof.

Far right, a hansom cab of 1873. Fast and elegant, these vehicles, introduced in the 1850s, were the taxis of Victorian London.

Below, King's Cross Station, built
1851–52 by Lewis Cubitt. A simple,
two-arched building, it contrasts
with its fantastic neo-Gothic
neighbour, St Pancras.

Right, a scene at Waterloo Station
(about 1870) recording the bustle
of a great railway terminus at a
time when rail travel was universal
among all classes both for long
and short journeys.

Top right, an express train at King's Cross in the 1890s. The engine is one of the famous 'Stirling Singles' (a reference to the huge centre wheel) of the Great Northern Railway, which were celebrated for their fast runs to the north.

Bottom right, Finchley Road Station in 1860, its rural surroundings soon to be engulfed in the approaching sprawl of London.

Far right, a Pullman dining car on the Great Northern Railway in 1879, where pampered passengers might dine in comfort, strictly segregated from less fortunate second- and third-class travellers.

Below, Tower Bridge being built. The bridge, one of London's landmarks, is still worked by the same hydraulic machinery used at its opening in 1894.

Right, unloading at London Docks in 1893. Though the Thames was no longer used for public transport (except for trippers), London was a thriving port whose docks were rebuilt to accommodate the huge new steamships.

A class at Sidney Road Primary School in 1901. Primary education became compulsory in 1870 and free for all children in 1891.

Art and learning

The spread of culture in the reign of Victoria coincided with the upsurge of the middle classes and their efforts to create a new educational system to serve the needs of an urban population. Previously, culture had belonged exclusively to the privileged aristocracy, whose sons had been educated in the classics at Westminster, Eton or Harrow before proceeding to Oxford and Cambridge, while boys of less exalted parentage went to the grammar schools and village children picked up the rudiments of reading and writing at the dame schools attached to their local vicarage. Some poor boys got their chance by obtaining scholarships to the Merchant Taylors' School, the Charterhouse or to St Paul's, which moved from the City in 1884 to a palatial Gothic structure erected by Alfred Waterhouse in the fields of Hammersmith. Some charity schools, paid for by voluntary subscriptions, gave their pupils a good education, and in 1827 London University had been founded for the study of science.

But all this was not enough to serve the growing pressure of an industrialized society, though no government before Gladstone's in 1870 dared to tackle the problem of educating the masses on account of the bitter warfare between the Established Church and the Non-Conformists. Parliament, however, passed Gladstone's bill setting up new Board Schools under a national School Board; and for the first time girls as well as boys were considered eligible for some kind of elementary tuition, while a crusade for their higher education was waged by the pioneering Miss Emily Davies and Miss Frances Mary Buss.

Fortified with claret and biscuits, these two demure-looking ladies with a militant confidence in their cause appeared in person to give evidence before the gentlemen sitting on the Royal Commission of 1865 and so impressed them that the results were revolutionary. Miss Buss's North London Collegiate School for Ladies in Camden Town flourished while Miss Davies went on to Cambridge to become the founder of Girton, and at Holloway College the first students in the eighties found an escape from the day-to-day monotony of Victorian family life.

No longer content with a little drawing and painting at home, they yearned to use their brains. And those with less intellectual pretensions went off to domestic science and secretarial colleges. The emancipation of women had begun.

All this educational activity was stimulated by the spirit of enquiry set in motion by Prince Albert at the Great Exhibition and, after his death, the enormous profits which had accrued from the Exhibition were used to endow a massive series of buildings in Kensington celebrating the arts and sciences and open to the public free of charge. The Natural History Museum, built in the Romanesque style by Alfred Waterhouse, covered acres on the Cromwell Road after another temporary International Exhibition had been held there in 1862. The Victoria and Albert, equally massive and filled with marvellous objects of all kinds, was designed by Captain Francis Fowke, who was also the architect of the Royal Albert Hall, built on the site of Lady Blessington's orchard. Indeed, all the dairy farms and market gardens of Brompton and South Kensington were transformed into a built-up area which included the Royal College of Music and the Royal College of Organists, the Imperial College of Science with its glorious tower designed by Colcutt and new streets in straight lines or immense blocks of flats to house the well-to-do middle classes.

The Prince Consort was responsible for their taste, and he was also responsible for the Queen's taste. In music she admired what he admired, as she did also in painting and sculpture. Soon after their marriage his seriousness had profoundly influenced the musical life of London. When he and the Queen appeared at the Royal Italian Opera House in Covent Garden, it was not to show themselves off and to laugh or chatter in their box, but to listen attentively to the inspired singing of Grisi, Mario and Tamburini in the operas of Rossini, Donizetti and Bellini; and when the Royal Opera House was burnt to the ground in 1856, the Prince immediately sponsored the building of a splendid new theatre on the site. At Buckingham Palace the Prince invited Mendelssohn to accompany the

Queen on the organ, and the composer's great oratorio *Elijah* was performed at the Exeter Hall in the Strand in their presence. After the Prince's death, his taste prevailed among the audiences at the St James's Hall in Piccadilly and the Queen's Hall, Langham Place, where the first Promenade Concerts were given in the nineties.

In painting and sculpture the Prince admired the pseudo-classical marbles of Thorneycroft and Theed, the large allegorical frescoes of Mr Uwins and above all the noble stags painted by Sir Edwin Landseer against a Scottish background of moorland and heather. The private view at the Royal Academy every summer was a social occasion. To be seen there, or better still, to be on nodding terms with the President, Sir Charles Eastlake, or with Mr Ruskin, the arbiter of Victorian taste, was to achieve the highest glory; and to stand in front of one's own portrait by Mr Watts or Sir John Everett Millais was most gratifying. The painters did well out of the snobs. Lord Leighton built himself a large mansion in Holland Park Road and Sir Lawrence Alma-Tadema a Renaissance palace in St John's Wood. Every picture told a story with a moral or a sentimental theme. Pre-Raphaelite ladies swooned among medieval lattice-work and Holman Hunt ploughed his religious furrow with exemplary zeal.

For those who could not afford to buy an oil-painting hanging at the Royal Academy, there were engravings and oleographs of the most popular pictures; Sir Edwin Landseer's *Dignity and Impudence* could be found artfully reproduced on the lid of a japanned coal-box. Culture at last was within reach of everybody engaged in the worthy pursuit of self-improvement. Even the poor were not forgotten. Free public libraries were started in some of the most impoverished London parishes; and reformers like John Cassell, who belonged to the National Temperance Society, began to publish weekly magazines called the *Teetotal Times* and the *Working Man's Friend* at 1d a copy, while for women there was *Eliza Cook's Journal*, the avowed purpose of the editress being 'to give her feeble aid to the gigantic struggle for elevation now going on among the working classes'.

Gradually the reading public was growing wider and more voracious. Samuel Orchard Beeton's *Englishwoman's Domestic Magazine* reached a sale over 50,000 copies a month. The *Illustrated London News* at 6d was the first periodical to commission black and white artists to illustrate world events; *Punch* was established in 1841 and Dickens the editor of *Household Words* in 1850. And in literature the Victorian period was an age of giants: of Tennyson, Browning and Elizabeth Barrett, imprisoned by sickness and a tyrannical father in Wimpole Street; of George Eliot, living in sin with George Henry Lewis on the north bank of the Regent's Canal, but so high-minded no one dared to criticize the irregularity of their union; of Charlotte Brontë, who came to London to visit her publisher having tricked him into believing he was going to meet a gentleman called Currer Bell; of Carlyle, the sage of Chelsea, Trollope living in Montagu Square, Thackeray, a Londoner by adoption; and of Dickens, the greatest of all Victorian Londoners, who roamed the streets by day and by night with his eyes and his ears and his whole soul awake to their lively character.

Dickens's unhappy childhood revealed to him all that was most wretched in the life of London—and he never forgot it, even when he became rich and successful and was living in his charming house in Devonshire Terrace, or enjoying a 'red-hot chop' at Jack Straw's Castle on Hampstead Heath. His books went round the world and his public readings in London and elsewhere were attended by wildly enthusiastic audiences. He wore beautiful shirts and jewelled tie-pins and liked showing himself off as an amateur actor. At forty-six he fell in love with a little actress the age of his eldest daughter and got a separation from his wife. When he died in 1870, Carlyle wrote: 'No death has fallen on me with such a stroke. The good, the gentle, high gifted, ever friendly and noble Dickens —every inch of him an honest man.'

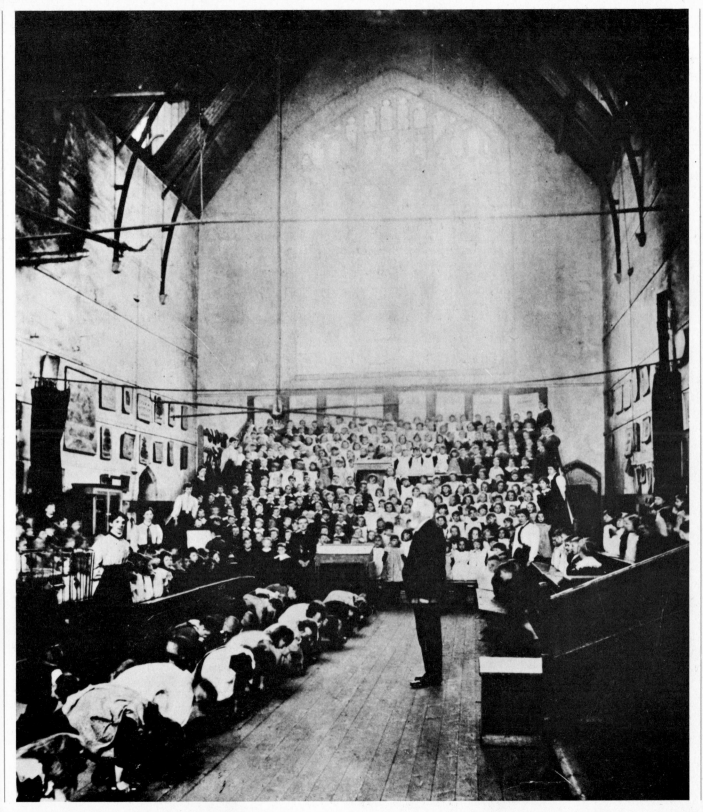

Top right, Brook Street 'Ragged'
School, one of several schools
run by the London City Mission
to teach the three Rs to destitute
and homeless children.

Bottom right, the schoolroom at
St Paul's in 1862, one of
London's oldest and best-known
schools, before it moved from
the City to Hammersmith.

Far right, two dolls in the
Bethnal Green Museum dressed as
Greencoat Charity School pupils.
Before the Education Act of 1870,
the schooling of working-class
children was largely left to
private religious charities.

Below, the Alexandra Palace, Muswell Hill, in 1875, the huge exhibition hall inspired by the Crystal Palace.

Right, the majolica fountain at the International Exhibition at South Kensington in 1862, where the Natural History Museum stands today. Proceeds from the Great Exhibition transformed the area around Exhibition Road into a complex of colleges and museums.

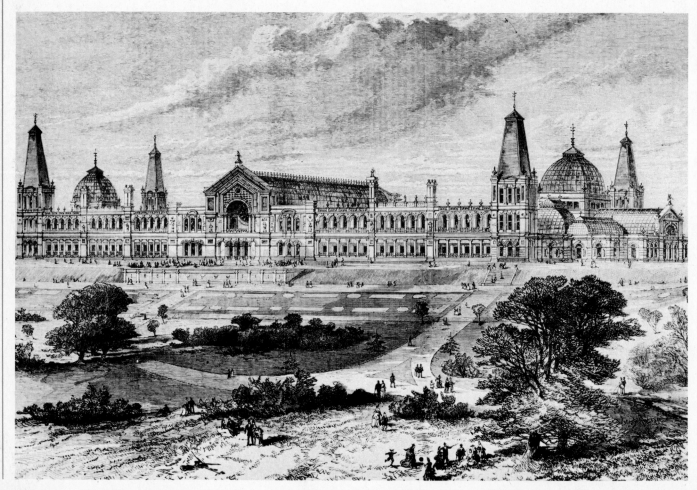

Four great Victorian writers:
right, Anthony Trollope; below,
Elizabeth Barrett Browning;
below right, George Eliot; and,
far right, Charles Dickens.

A cover to five cockney songs of Albert Chevalier, a famous star of late Victorian music hall.

Victorian amusements

In spite of their strong belief in the virtue of hard work and their close attention to the business of making money, the Victorians enjoyed their leisure with great gusto. The theatres flourished, the music halls rocked with hilarious laughter. Fun and frolic burst out on Bank Holidays at Hampstead Heath and Clapham Common; the pleasure-boats up and down the Thames were crowded with cockney boys and girls out for a lark. In the West End at night, the hansom cabs jingled in the streets and the gas lights blazed, while the man about town with his cane and his lavender gloves hunted his prey in Soho and the Haymarket. Life in London could be gay and raffish, or quiet and sober, according to the taste of the individual.

Queen Victoria and Prince Albert had decided soon after their marriage that it was their duty 'to elevate the drama from the low state it had fallen into'. Charles Kean was their favourite actor—he was such a gentleman and his wife, Ellen Tree, was such a lady, they were not at all like the rest of the theatrical profession. The Bancrofts, also, were a model of connubial respectability; and it was they who enticed polite society back into the theatre by cutting out the more debased forms of entertainment which for so long had appealed to the depraved taste of the *hoi polloi* and reducing the bill to a single piece, with perhaps a curtain raiser.

At the Lyceum, Henry Irving and Ellen Terry put new life into Shakespeare and the romatic melodramas that fitted Irving's style of acting so well; his dignified behaviour earned him the first knighthood ever to be bestowed on a member of the theatrical profession. At the same time the Gilbert and Sullivan operas, launched by D'Oyly Carte at the Savoy Theatre, established a new standard of musical entertainment, and night after night the theatre was filled with fashionable society. White ties and tails, diamonds and kid gloves were *de rigueur* in the orchestra stalls at the St James's Theatre also, where George Alexander's gentlemanly manner gave prestige to the society dramas of Wilde and Pinero while the more humble patrons in the gallery or the pit were equally thrilled by the acting of Mrs Patrick Campbell on the stage and the scenes from High Life in the auditorium.

But for the true Londoner by far the most popular form of entertainment was the music hall, which, in the midst of Victorian prudery and priggishness, offered a whole world of uninhibited fun drawn from the natural comic genius of the people and brewed up into a marvellous, ribald concoction of winkles and champagne, toffs and swells, giddy girls and pint-sized cockney comics. The halls ranged from the smallest, grubbiest 'free-and-easies' in the tavern saloons of Hoxton and Islington to the red-plush glitter of the Oxford and the Canterbury and the sophisticated splendour of the Empire in Leicester Square.

The artists were rich in talent and generous in giving. George Leybourne, with his dundreary whiskers, top hat and spats, made a fortune singing *Champagne Charlie* and spent it like water. Jenny Hill, the child of a cockney cab-driver, and Bessie Bellwood, who started as a rabbit-skinner in the New Cut, both burnt themselves out at around the age of forty. The incomparable Dan Leno, with his little wizened face and wistful smile, had genius. Albert Chevalier's cockney songs were whistled in the streets and sung in drawing-rooms. Marie Lloyd, after her giddy climb up the ladder from the Grecian Saloon in the City Road, via Hoxton, Bermondsey and the Old Mo' in Drury Lane, was Queen of the Halls in the nineties, her feathered hats and frilly dresses, nods and winks and saucy smiles adored equally by the boys in the gallery and the posh gentlemen in the stalls.

Indeed the London music halls were a great leveller in Victorian society. Respectable women stayed away from them, but the bowler-hatted clerks and their doxies rubbed shoulders with the Bohemian *literati* and the man about town in search of dissipation and pleasure. Oscar Wilde and Aubrey Beardsley were to be seen haunting the Oxford and the Empire, when not sitting at the marble-topped tables in the gilt and plush glitter of the Café Royal. And although the whole gaudy bubble of Wilde's reputation was pricked like an air balloon by his trail and subsequent imprisonment, the Philistines in art who deplored his sin as 'a crime more horrible than murder' were fighting a losing battle against the doctrine of Art for Art's sake and could not entirely ignore the devotees of the Aesthetic Movement.

This so-called Movement had grown out of two distinct branches of artistic aspiration: the Pre-Raphaelite Brotherhood consisting of Rossetti and his followers and the new Bohemianism adopted by Whistler and Algernon Swinburne. Whistler had utterly defeated Ruskin as the high priest of Victorian taste in art in 1878 and had introduced Rossetti to the Parisian craze for collecting blue-and-white china, which spread to the drawing-rooms of Chelsea and Kensington. Swinburne had shocked the conventional bourgeoisie by his romantic approach to 'the pleasures of sin' in his lurid *Poems and Ballads*, and Wilde as a young undergraduate new to London, had carried the idea of 'a pleasure that was poisonous' to excess. He gloried in the decadence and the corruption of the movement and it destroyed him; yet his influence, by exploding the myth of Victorian sobriety, excited a whole section of London society to reject the moral prohibitions of the middle classes.

They, of course, were loud in their condemnation. They knew what they liked in the way of pleasure: their annual outing to the Christmas pantomime at Drury Lane, a visit to the Crystal Palace in the summer or to the Zoo. The Crystal Palace had been re-erected at Sydenham and was used for choral concerts and exhibitions, marvellous firework displays in the grounds, archery meetings and balloon ascents. The Zoological Gardens in Regent's Park were founded for the serious, scientific study of wild animal life, but were charming as well as instructive, though Fanny Horsley, the sister-in-law of Brunel, thought the monkeys were 'very indelicate'. There were elephant rides for the children and

*Marie Lloyd, who with her
extravagant clothes and saucy
manner, captivated the audiences
at the Old Mo', Drury Lane.*

buns for the bears, except on Sundays when only the Fellows of the Society were allowed in.

But the cockneys got fun out of watching their 'betters' enjoying themselves. They admired the rich, sporting gentlemen who revived the glories of the Coaching Club, and turned out to watch them in Hyde Park. They enjoyed the cricket at Lord's and staring at the toffs and the fashionable ladies. They went off to Putney and Mortlake to cheer the crews of the Oxford and Cambridge Boat Race; and in the great frost of 1895, they slid across the ice in St James's Park and fell on their backsides at the feet of the elegant ladies and gentlemen on skates.

They had curiosity, vitality and wit. They loved the Easter Fairs at Chelsea Bridge and Greenwich, the street musicians and the acrobats. They liked their garish, frowsty pubs smelling of beer and gin and cheap tobacco, but they liked the rural surroundings of the Bull and Bush just as well, the donkey rides on Hampstead Heath and paddling in the ponds. They liked being photographed all in a bunch, or just walking about in couples, the girls with their skirts trailing in the grass and the boys in their city suits. On the river they watched the ladies with their sunshades and the gentlemen in boating caps punting upstream with their picnic baskets, and as an outing for themselves, loved the oily engine smell, the uproar and the crush of the pleasure-steamers to Southend or Richmond. And in the nineties they had fun gaping at the ladies in straw boaters and boots to hide their ankles as they rode their new bicycles in Battersea Park.

The bicycle was a symbol of freedom. It marked the end of an era and the beginning of a new century in London. The stuffiness, the rectitude, much of the poverty and some of the glamour were soon to vanish in the dramatic events of a future the Victorians had never been able to conceive. But acres of London remained, a monument to their firm belief in progress and to their development of the most powerful capital city in the world.

Right, Ellen Terry, queen of the late Victorian theatre and co-star with Irving in Shakespeare at the Lyceum Theatre.

Far right, a charity matinee at the Haymarket Theatre in 1899. By the end of Victoria's reign, the theatre, after its long domination by melodrama, had become 'serious' and respectable.

Right, Sir Henry Irving in
The Bells *(1871), the first of his*
long series of brilliant
productions at the Lyceum.

Far right, the 'three little maids'
in The Mikado, *one of Gilbert and*
Sullivan's wildly popular light
operas.

Top right, Aubrey Beardsley, the brilliant black-and-white illustrator and, with Wilde, a follower of the new Bohemianism.

Bottom right, a cover design by Beardsley for The Yellow Book (of which he was art editor). It was withdrawn after Beardsley's dismissal because of the Wilde scandal.

Far right, Oscar Wilde, high priest of decadence and the creed of art for art's sake. Before his disgrace, he enlivened the theatre with a series of witty comedies.

Below, a drawing of Newmarket Races, a favourite gathering-place of London society, showing the Prince of Wales indulging in two favourite sports: racing and talking to pretty women.

Right, Dr. W. G. Grace among the spectators at Lord's in 1891. Cricket was better organized and more generally played than any other sport.

Below, strolling in Hyde Park and watching the leaders of fashion ride by in their smart carriages – a favourite afternoon amusement.

Right, a crowd of young (and not-so-young) boys gather round a stall at Chelsea Bridge Road Fair in 1890. Much popular amusement was found in the streets in this age before the motor car.

123

Top right, the Crystal Palace at Sydenham about 1888, where it was re-erected after the Great Exhibition to provide continuous entertainment and instruction.

Bottom right, skating at St James's Park in the bitterly cold winter of 1895.

Far right, an elephant ride in Regent's Park Zoo in 1900. The Zoo was a popular place for Victorian family outings.

Below, keen bicyclists line up
before setting off for a ride. The
arrival of the bicycle marked a
new era of mobility and freedom,
especially for women.

Right, boating on the Thames at
Richmond in the 1890s. Trips on
the river were one of many
pastimes that became more widely
enjoyed with the increase of
leisure and prosperity.

PICTURE SOURCES

Figures refer to page numbers
Aerofilms Ltd., 32; Bethnal Green Museum 61,97; Brighton Art Gallery, 118(B); G.L.C. Photo Library, 87, 91; London Transport Board, 72; Mansell Collection, 33, 42, 48, 60, 64, 66, 78(T), 82, 126; Museum of British Transport, 78(B); Radio Times Hulton Picture Library, all jacket photos, 4, 8, 13, 14, 15, 16, 17, 18, 19, 20, 21, 22, 23, 24, 25, 26, 38, 43, 53, 54, 55, 56, 57, 58, 59, 62, 63, 65, 67, 68, 70, 71, 77, 81, 82(T), 83, 84, 85, 86, 88, 89, 95, 96, 98, 99, 100, 101, 102, 104, 105, 106, 107, 108, 113, 114, 115, 116, 117, 118(T), 119, 120, 121, 122, 123, 124, 125, 127; George Rodger photographs, 36, 37, 46, 61, 80, 97, 103; Michael Taylor photographs, 34, 35, 39, 40, 41, 44, 45; Harold White photograph, 69; Peter Sullivan, map, 31

SOME FAMOUS VICTORIAN PHOTOGRAPHERS

JOHN THOMSON (1837–1921). Photographs on pages 4, 38, 43, 48, 64, 71, 79. Scottish photographer and explorer, principally known for his *Street Life in London* (1877), a documentary record of working-class life.

PAUL MARTIN (1864–1942). Photographs on jacket back, pages 123, 125, 127. 'Candid cameraman' of London street scenes in the 1890s, which he photographed with a concealed camera.

W. & D. DOWNEY. Photograph on page 24. Established a photographic studio in 1856. Early in their career they became patronized by royalty and prominent figures in society, politics and the arts.

ROGER FENTON (1819–96). Photographs on jacket back flap, page 15. A lawyer by profession, Fenton spent eleven years as a photographer, notably of the Crimean War. His work also includes landscapes, portraits and a fine series of cathedrals and sculptures.

Picture research by Doris Bryen
Designed by Rodney Springett for
London Weekend Television Publications

A